THE RHYTHM OF LIFE

Poetry

Ngozi Olivia Osuoha

Edited by Andrew Nyongesa
cover art by Ngozi Olivia Osuoha

Mwanaka Media and Publishing Pvt Ltd,
Chitungwiza Zimbabwe
*

Creativity, Wisdom and Beauty

i

Publisher: Mmap
Mwanaka Media and Publishing Pvt Ltd
24 Svosve Road, Zengeza 1
Chitungwiza Zimbabwe
mwanaka@yahoo.com
www.africanbookscollective.com/publishers/mwanaka-media-and-publishing
https://facebook.com/MwanakaMediaAndPublishing/

Distributed in and outside N. America by African Books Collective
orders@africanbookscollective.com
www.africanbookscollective.com

ISBN: 978-1-77929-607-8
EAN: 9781779296078

DISCLAIMER
All views expressed in this publication are those of the author and
do not necessarily reflect the views of *Mmap*.

iii

DEDICATION

To my wonderful parents Mr. and Mrs. B. A. Osuoha and my siblings.

Also to my primary school, National School, Nkwerre. The first place of formal learning I stepped my feet as a beginner.

ACKNOWLEDEMENT

I heartily appreciate all my primary and secondary school teachers. They were my ladder, without them I would not have been able to read or write. May God bless each and all of them, may He grant the dead perfect rest in His beautiful paradise.
I love you all, unquantifiable.
Also I thank Engr Echefu Ekene S. for technically restoring this piece.

TABLE OF CONTENTS

INTRODUCTION

THE RHYTHM OF LIFE is a book written in rhyme, with sixty five chapters, probably the first of its kind.It talks about life and its rhyme, the rhythm and melody, of how to be in harmony in a catastrophic, noisy and nuisance-filled world.

The Rhythm Of Life is a tool carefully fashioned to live in tune, tone and line in a constantly changing musical world. As if, it all about music. The frequency, pitch and keys of the worldly keyboard; Living here requires an instrumentalist who is devoted to his instruments, be they musical or not. Well laid out plans, insights, resonances, and dance steps, trying to show the dancer how to man the dancefloor and the stage, in order to be a wonderful performer.

This book hammers on wrong notes, poor dances, hard influences and bad rhythms killing the resonances of life. One needs, the dancer especially, which is the human and humans in question, to be properly enlightened on tunes of life, in order to sing and or dance along in a very melodious manner.

A good singer can make a good dancer, but when one hardly sings or dances, one tend to perform woefully in a world of performing artists.

Life is a stage, we perform, we leave, good or bad, with or without ovation. But it matters that we leave with ovation, especially when it is high.

It is aimed at teaching, reaching, correcting, enlightening, helping, directing and redirecting the living to find their feet in this slippery and aged world.

This introduction is purely in musical terms, depicting the name "THE RHYTHM OF LIFE"

CHAPTER 1:
THE HIM

I never enjoyed his cane
Today, it is my sugarcane,
I thought he was strict
But he built me a district,
He went to the extreme
Just to make me supreme
To me, it was affliction
But truly an affection,
He taught me also the negative
Preparing me for the positive,
I never really understood
Today, it is my livelihood,
He was not a millionaire
But richer than a billionaire
A seasoned educationist
Generational philanthropist,
Never went to teach with note
Because he was not remote,
The ground is filled with seed
The world will never lack feed
He is a set of tools
And a pure wonder to fools,
Not interested in fame
Rather in good name
Not a modern preacher
Old and excellent teacher
Not embittered by scandals
Changed many rascals,
Never intimidated by number
Neither went into slumber,

His voice, an echo
To the walls of Jericho
Never believed in cowardice
That was a natural choice,
Respects every man
Except those that rotate like fan,
He teaches many, far and near
And tames all their fear,
Befriends those in leprosy
Not falling for jealousy,
He loves the Navy
And so hates envy
His advice is the best
If God would do the rest,
He has the grace
To keep things in place
Some gather to pull him down
But he could die for his crown,
He really fits the world
His wisdom, from God
A friend without class
Especially to those in the glass
From sports, he built sportsmanship
He puts it in every relationship,
He is a great legend
That will know no end,
Everyday is his remembrance
For he is the real substance,
I pity, the unborn
May see not his horn
Or see him in person
But must learn his lesson,
When he goes to his root
Though not on bare foot,

He will go to his creator
Who made him contractor.
Many write their names on the ground
Clean them when they turn around,
He wrote his in the sky
There, those with wings fly,
He has the experience
And great intelligence,
A soldier, so brave
Always wanting to save
Never afraid of any situation
For permanent is no condition,
Trained, climbed by his sweat
Not a president, but great
Leaders need him always
For he carries light rays
They run to him for knowledge
All these they acknowledge,
Cares less about mockery
And forgets about treachery,
Wanting to put the house in order
Even with all their murder,

CHAPTER 2:
LISTEN

Stay away from trouble
In order not to wobble,
Instead be on your own
Even if you are fully blown,
You can seek for aid
And also can get paid,
The world that is rolling away
Hold not on the clay
Inside this very ship
Someone holds a whip,
It is to correct injustice
For there has been a notice,
He has no challenger
And he is not a stranger,
The time comes fast
Already there is a forecast
Let the evil doer repent
Though you live in golden tent,
Stand up for your faith
Hear what God saith
Soon, no more dying
Keep the news flying,
Someday it shall be a rest
To all who have been on test,
Our words are not always true
They can bring a rescue,
For the bees in their hive
It matters how they live,
If they have you to harass
Sure, you they will embarrass,
I tell you this for a purpose

To save your nose,
When you see them, be quick
Never scatter them with stick,
My good friend Thompson
Had a brother Jackson,
Both play football
Their kid sister, basketball
Their children hang out a lot
Which makes open the dot,
All can spend one million
Forcing them into rebellion,
What matters is not the passport
Rather the capability and effort,
On the dawn of their inventory
It can be a negative history
So it is not good to slumber
Even if you are a plumber.
Some people ride on the poor
Shutting them behind the door,
Though not the best option
Because it creates some fraction
Though it was civilization
That served as neutralization,
With the advent of Christianity
We strive for maturity
Unfortunately, we are deaf
And lighter than the leaf,
Standing to our feet
Opens fresh sheet,
That the world to come
May be at home
Learn from the Psalmist
He was a moralist,
He was zealous

And God jealous,
So, He remains through time
Whether we, old or prime
Helping one get to climax
Where he may relax,
Though we can feel weary
In the way, tearful and dreary
For something dear
One may tend to bear,
Because life is an errand
In this strange land.
Sometimes those that mock
Are under some lock,
So they open their mouth
Crossing the south,
If you have your opinion
As your only companion,
Soon you will freeze
With little breeze,
We have poem to write
Though we hate sprite,
If he is controversial
And equally racial,
If he enjoys in Dublin
He may not play the violin,
He that bears Delano
May not die for the piano,
Not that he hates it
But for him not to quit.
In the beginning of anarchy
Everything loses its hierarchy.

CHAPTER 3:
REALITY

Having lost the real sum
It will not be funny to Mum,
Especially after putting her best
And hoping to meet the request.
Many wonder why they fail
At the point of getting bail,
Not what they deserve
But some hot tea to serve
For one that is crying
May not really be dying,
Watch a man of passion
He excels in his mission,
Study those who kill
Nothing gives them, fill
They are always miserable
And their children, terrible
No good note they leave
They only bereave
Give them double barrel
Allow them the quarrel,
Look into their dictionary
They send many to mortuary,
Around them is the coward
Not that he is wayward,
But he wants to escape
Instead of seeing a rape
Their true colour is red
To recall they that bled,
Visitations that are angelic
Look wonderful like magic,
It can never be hidden

Even in the garden of Eden,
Many a time, people faint
When covered with paint,
This makes them frown
And certain times lose their crown
Never you darken the kettle
If you are cooking some beetle
Allow things to manifest
They may bring good harvest
Seeds must germinate
Never try to terminate,
Once again, do not hurt
Whether or not you are short,
Those we kill and murder
Draw spiritual border,
Watch it, there is a line
Where none can be fine,
A king equally is human
Everyone is a man
We can wear a fitted suit
In all our daily pursuit,
This does not go too long
Farther or higher than our song,
Our robes tell little
They do not fit the battle,
Our minds do the conquest
Everything lies on our chest,
Let nothing roll you away
For the treasure is on the tray,
Turn back, have it if you wish
It may turn a big fish,
Learn from the children
Assuming you are a Sanhedrin,
Nobody is perfect

Hence they are imperfect,
Life is thrilling and confusing
Sometimes funny and amusing,
Answers are nowhere
And enemies; everywhere.

CHAPTER 4:
WATCH

The head is the chief
He himself is the thief,
Forget not the story
It is part of history,
But never cook a lie
It may come back to tie
Not too long it will be reached
Including those we bleached,
Call him weeping Jeremiah
Name him a resounding Isaiah,
The truth is the message
Very plain on the page,
Always study the Bible
It is like golden marble,
Nothing falls to the ground
They all are found,
Those who turn back
Finally turn too black,
If nothing is being done
They are totally gone,
Listen, rise up again
It will stop the pain
Though may not be soon
Sure, up there is the moon.
The world is not artificial
But we made it superficial,
Those who shoot are wicked
Their ways too, crooked
Return, and stay healthy
Invest and grow wealthy,
Just tighten your belt

Your waist shall not melt
Wake up and revive
Eat well and survive,
Water will not finish
Bread may not diminish
Around the earth is corn
You are just a new born
All will help you live
So never mind to forgive
A lamb is not a goat
Please wear him a coat,
Life is about sacrifice
It is the only thing nice,
Hearken, do not be deceived
I know you have believed,
Tomorrow comes a fool
Softer than some wool
But I tell you again now
Let your knees never bow,
When you must shout
Do not just walk out
Let them hear your voice
It may be the only choice,
Those in the darkness
Know nothing of happiness,
Liberate them for joy
Buy them fine toy
Freedom is coming ahead
See it above your head,
Open your mouth, declare
That you may have your share
Take good and fitted chair
Make it worthy and fair,
Rejoice, the world is ending

The Lord has her heart mending
Pour away the evil oil
Bury it on the bad soil
Spread your hands for peace
Wear beautiful mouth piece,
Prepare well to enjoy
God is sending an envoy

CHAPTER 5:
STAY ALERT

Before now, it was not so
Men had nowhere to go
But they were not worried
Because they were buried,
Now is the time of salvation
God is reaching each nation
Hearken to the wilderness voice
Lest you make the wrong choice,
Believe the news, the message
Before you end in the cage,
Ask others, they saw light
And were given the might
Come, denounce torture
Flee, be set for rapture,
I tell you this, to announce
Not for you to renounce,
Proclaim the tidings of Zion
Fail not like the lion
Good reward awaits all
Who continue to stand tall,
If you deny your throne
The blame is your own
Put it on none again
For Jesus made it plain
Those who read Biology
Not superior to psychology
Humble yourself and learn
Make it a big concern,
Knowledge is the map
Wisdom bridges the gap
Zeal is the conqueror

Vision, the emperor,
Determination is lubricant
Victory, the true want,
Anger a turning point
Failure; dislocated joint
Discouragement's an isolator
Trials need a facilitator,
The heat reveals the star
Shakings unfold the superstar
Mountains are the indicator
Fountains water the victor,
Wickedness demotes the tyrant
Uneasiness grabs the militant
Ahead is the narrow gate
Ongoing is a big debate
Surely, there is a winner
He may be thinner,

CHAPTER 6:
THE TRUTH

Locked up is a giant
Free is the tiniest ant
Crawling is an athlete
It is amazingly concrete
In the morning, it was shining
Now it is wearing a lining
Someone knows the whole truth
But he is waiting for Ruth
He fears like Gideon
Praying to bear Simeon
In the beginning, it was not so
Everybody knew what to do
Later everything went wrong
And the old buried the young,
All things are now sour
Despite who makes the tour
Cut off the bitterness
It will develop to illness
And the top, there is a crane
We can name it Jane,
If there is a survivor
Then there is a successor
Listen again for awhile
This matter may be fragile
Let those who fight be ready
Not necessarily with some Brandy
The heart is the throne of victory
Time is the page of history
Our children must not sleep
That we may not weep,
This fight is for the future

I can see clearly the picture
Those who belittle you are not better
Just that they have some butter,
The bread we eat is not choosy
It does not know where is rosy
They grab much and enough
As others hunger and cough
Any sane man is sound
So he can easily be found,
But those who steal are crazy
They do because they are lazy
One to stand, he needs support
He must not work in a seaport
Around the work are heroes
Most die like tomatoes
I have seen a Peter
Who is always bitter
He has a good fishing net
He prays some catch to get
But not as easy as that
Even in things we are good at,
Life is baffling and questionable
And tremendously incredible
For the more you deserve
The less you have to reserve,
At first it looks bright
Midway you remain right
Suddenly, you come crashing
Lightening, keep flashing
Nobody has the solution
So they go for evolution,
The fantasy becomes illusion
Harder appears the conclusion
Therefore declare at liberty

Let all hold unto his property
At least, for the moment
That may end the lament,
Again, I tell you be smart
It may mean for one to part

CHAPTER 7:
NOTHING IS NEW

On the contrary, life continues
But everything discontinues
Children play without trouble
They believe their needs are double
Each time they have their want
So they mess on their pant
Their worry is nothing
Their plight is something,
These children are very free
They can stand like a tree
You must be careful
It is indeed needful
You may lie on the table
But write on the marble
Else you would be forgotten
And your name rotten,
The ladder we climb is bent
Rough, rugged, others went
Be vigilant, lest you slip
Your steps, you can flip
The third world is sleeping
While the cold is creeping,
The undeveloped is battered
While others have chattered,
Sound loud the trumpet
Pray well your chaplet
Announce the return of slavery
This is only for the bravery
The master is still awake
Holding firm his rake,
Yet the servant is resting

Allowing the birds, nesting
The writing is interpreted
The mission is intended,
Both are on the race
It may not be on their face
Surely one remains at the back
And he shall always lack
A wise man is diligent
He too is very intelligent
Weigh the sword of the viper
Heavier than that of the piper,
The former is a fighter
The latter; an entertainer
Pushing on is a winning tip
Singing on; shouting tip

CHAPTER 8:
TAKE YOUR TIME

Not too good to rush
Put down the brush
Stand near and look back
There is a big crack
Building the future on the mat
Only attracts the biggest rat,
People who delight in evil
Hardly become better or civil
Though they grow for awhile
Presenting, carrying great file
Not many know the content
And the distance they went,
True, they wear an apparel
That may not cause a quarrel
Watch them they are bold
On their neck are fine gold
Turn around and feel secure
You need no more cure,
Jump up on your feet
If there is somewhere to meet
I tell you they look good
And they have some food,
Believe it you will soon cry
Because they will leave you dry
They are gone with the morning
And you are there, burning
Once more, about your pocket
It will fly like a rocket
Watch they are not too far
But there is a big bar
If you venture fighting across

You will be a heavy loss
Focus on your life again
This remains on the plain
Never build on some lust
Only be fair and just,
Otherwise life is fragile
Whether or not you are agile
I have seen them murder
Yet they remain on the ladder,
These people have nothing to suffer
Instead they give and offer
Good, better and best
They have sweet rest
Bad, worse and worst
They can never burst,
Their fear is normal death
Their pride is their wealth.

CHAPTER 9:
NOTHING TO OFFER

I wonder deep their strength
Because I know they get to length
Very tempted are they that watch
For they have nothing to catch,
Under my head is a roof
Below my feet, some proof
I just cannot understand
The number of their band,
I baffle and get confused
At the little they have refused
Not really their choice
For they have good rice,
They sleep not on the bed
Because they hardly wed
I am weakened when I think
It makes me to sink
How one can be alone
When he has a fat bone
Sure, life itself is empty
And we learn not plenty
The totality of it is greed
Some made it their creed,
A few see it as rosary
Many call it a misery
Believe or not, it's real
It has a big seal
Men descend to the grave
With good or bad wave,
Inside the pit is a friend
It is nothing but the end
Enemies fight and loot

Friends march just on foot,
You will see them fight
For the lack of sight
Because they reap without sowing
Someday I see it overflowing,
Talk to them or not
They have put the dot
So you waste your energy
For you are the allergy,
Pick up your bow and leave
Let them gather and weave
There is an appointed time
When there shall be no crime,
The world now and today
Moving and giving way
Soon, it shall be fired
It is old and tired.

CHAPTER 10:
HOLD THIS

Even the ordinary tip
Will close like zip
For soon all will be fine
With none passing the line,
From time, it has been
Many people have seen
Yet many never know
This must surely blow
Let those who killed, mourn
And they that strayed, return
The danger must withdraw
Because God is much raw
These men care less for good
They deeply endanger fatherhood
Unconcerned, they march forward
Undefeated, they return rightward
Their voice echoes like earthquake
As they eat and chew their cake
Blood! Blood! They shout
This is what we truly bet
I fear someone there, is weak
He wants to crash the peak,
When I have a dream born
I beautify it with ribbon
For it to be very attractive
Then, I am being creative
Guard good things you nurture
Let nothing them; puncture
The mystery of faith is a weapon,
Fill it like some coupon
Be mindful of who you are

Take heed and much care,
Make your wishes, the subject
Build them like a new project
Wanting to do more not less
Let nothing stain your dress,
This again is very important
Use your trunk like an elephant
Wherever you go, take a glue
For you to stick to the clue,
Otherwise, you may lose the guide
Especially at wave and tide
Anything, you cannot cook
You must not lose the book,
So gather now your strength
Go for all at length

CHAPTER 11:
MAKE SURE YOU LEARN

Listen to the radio
Learn more about polio
Chase it as far as possible
Remember nothing is impossible,
If you hinder yourself now
You may never learn how
I do not want any mark
Instead I go for good remark,
The things we love or keep
Determine whether we may weep
About this time yesterday
Somebody died on the way,
Sure, we must someday bow
But better for some to say wow!
Our favour is not steady
So look for a good remedy
Because when you are all alone
Jesus may not want to atone,
There is one thing I have learnt
It is what God actually meant
Draw near to Him and close
There, is for your life a purpose,
Wander and stay far away
You lose and mourn all day
Away from the pain we added
Everything was really padded,
No divination against you
No enchantment going through
Just give up and let go
You have nothing to forgo,
Hear this, God loves all

Answer now, His good call.
We can boast of tears
We can never avoid fears
So, return and have rest
You can end the struggle
If you come to God and mingle,
The world is just a block
With indeed a heavy lock
Things go zig zag
They run into some fag
For the man, Larry
He has much to carry,
Show him the road
He limps like a toad
I wonder where he goes
Perishing just like tomatoes.

CHAPTER 12:
RISE UP

I have my own creed
It is not about greed
I write my own anthem
It is my royal diadem
I do too my song
Sometimes, short or long,
They tell a whole lot
Reminding me when and not
Believe or not, doubt it
I know where I can sit
My eyes can see a little
But God can also rekindle,
They did terrible ills
But He can foot the bills
I got my toes crushed
But my blood never flushed,
The day of God will be wonderful
Those bruised will be beautiful
What I learnt in the class
I shall not lose in the glass
Many want me to suffer
That, I do not prefer,
Others want me dead
But they shall welcome me made
I have gone to hell
God preserved my cell,
I visited the grave
God guarded the wave
I jumped into the lagoon
He enveloped me like balloon,
I fainted and passed away

He revived me in one day
I died and lost it all
God still made me tall
I have seen affliction
More than their prediction
I have been roasted for meal
But God did not strike their deal
What on earth have I not seen?
Which part of hell have I not been?
Yet many prayed more for me
Others wished much more for me,
As meek as I am
Quiet, cool and calm
Yet they wanted me dead
They fixed a thorn on my head,
Something only Jesus did
None said God forbid
They hated me so angrily
They wished me evil so hungrily
A world made up of men
It is nothing but a den
Written boldly on their face
They win it like a race
As though it is an award
Or some heavenly reward
Brothers hate you most
People ridicule your host,
If you want to succeed in life
Put down the sword or knife
Because they lead to nowhere
Mostly if you wish to get somewhere
Let nothing trouble your heart
Even the world of science and art,
I tell you forget luxury

Neither go for pain nor penury
But keep your head high
Sure, you must really sigh
Sometimes, you have to cry
It does not mean you must fry
Those who brighten up cope
Even when there is no hope.

CHAPTER 13:
DO NOT HATE BACK

Life grows like plantain
With a lot to retain
Watch just the flowers
You will believe the showers
Though troubles abound
They too return to ground
Because God is near to fight
When we tell Him our plight
Once or several it will hit
It can leave us bit by bit
Yet those who are stronger
Have to wait for longer,
I tell you to wear hard
That you play well your card
Failing to do just that
Will lie you on the mat
There is some work to be done
And you need not to be gone,
Whether or not you are fragile
Make yourself ready and agile
You have to run and fly
Because your place is in the sky
The world is too choosy
But not and never rosy,
Sleep on ordinary floor
Hang on the door
They neither care nor mind
But when you glow, they find
I have told you this again
Rely not always on gain
Some losses teach good lesson

It does not matter your person
Crave for things that are good
Far and outside the neighbourhood,
Please be loving and caring
You know not who you are rearing
Friend, president or angel
Goat, shepherd or rebel
Be soft, hard and gentle
Finely position your mantle
Here, we have counterfeit
There are some to forfeit
Yes, we have also heroes
They taste like mangoes
Replacement, not by willingness
More of humility and fitness,
Touch people when you should
Forget them not for you could,
They too can rise any moment
And be a better resident
Some people become adamant
When the need is rampant,
I hear the cry of people
It moves like a big ripple
I feel the pain of children
Yoked like some brethren
A wedge is holding the sphere
Not the best atmosphere
We would have some peace
If we remain in piece
Troubleshooting is not the issue
Instead it scatters the tissue
A bond exists between three
But more holds a perfect tree
Think deep and understand

Bother not the blue band
A crowd is springing forth
It will pass the fourth
Sure, every man to his tent
Whether far or near they went
There is a road to destruction
Another, unknown to construction.

CHAPTER 14:
STOOP AND CONQUER

No man knows everything
A fool knows something
Those who are in the front,
May lack the courage to confront
Watch those at the back
Some have nothing to lack,
The arrow can hurt or pierce
Men can also face it fierce
Make your troubles low
Keep them too in a row
So that you can attack each
When they come to preach,
If you are always sad
Try and make yourself glad
Lay aside the weight of anger
Let it never be a hunger
Because it comes with boredom
It ceases your peace and freedom,
Grab your paper and pen
Even if your name is not Ben
Write down your joy
Let it neither stop nor cloy,
The environment is calling hatred
Are you going to paint it red?
We must reach a resolution
If we are avoiding revolution
The ladder is not strong
Climbing might be wrong
When we approach the fall
We kick back our ball
I have called you Ephraim

Make sure you bury each claim
Be humble and submissive
If your work is to go massive,
There is one out there appointed
Someone up there got him anointed
Clean up your nose
Absolutely nothing will you lose
Handle well the delicate egg
Do not break it with a peg
Carefulness will save you some trouble
I tell you this is not a gamble
If you cannot bear a yoke
Then soon you will choke,
Wash the goat, bath the pig
They are meat too big
Forget the horror of last night
Now you have a better sight,
As you try to keep mute
None will hear your flute,
The children want to dance
Halt them not from your distance
Bear the touch of wisdom
Submit also to heirdom
I warn you, life is short
Anywhere can be a port
Now listen to the noises
They carry and make choices
Each sound is a note
You can make it a keynote
Any interval you choose to sing
There is something you must bring
That is primarily your voice
It can make people rejoice
At a pitch you can stop

If you feel on the top
But remember life can be dark
So you do not have to bark,
Make a point, strike the balance
Though just at a glance
Many watch, many are bright
Failed, they win the fight.

CHAPTER 15:
THINK TWICE

It is worthwhile to rest
Even when going to the west,
Granted, it is a necessity
But not an impossibility,
Let your hands get busy
Make your head less lazy
Otherwise issues will germinate
And troubles gradually emanate,
If you must be a fool
It does not mean dying in the pool
The time is fast going
You must be fast running,
Break down the thick fence
It will be a great evidence
In the night when you sleep
Think hard and really deep,
Wake up in freshness
It will bring happiness
When starting a new day
Let anxiety just stay
Pull them away and relax
Let them melt like wax,
They that surround your camp
Can never put your lamp
Be still and take courage
It will be another advantage,
Rest assured, it keeps coming
Strong like never before, keep moving
I am not a sermonist
Neither am I a scientist,
But I do my little great

Then it becomes a big threat
As I avoid the enemy-battalion
I try not to be a dead lion,
It could be misleading
Though I dream of leading
Somebody can touch the mark
It does not mean it is filthy
But that person is guilty.
Life can give us a flower
It may be higher than a tower
Look at it deep and well
Press the button or bell
Give it out there and once
Then it will reach a distance
Troubles last and fade away
Problems knock day by day

CHAPTER 16:
A NEW BEGINNING

They look old and new
Our strength tend to renew
If you gather the harvest
Without building a nest,
As big as it may be
Much you may not see
Look around and draw the line
Weigh it and be sure it is fine,
Under those shoes you wear
There is a sound you cannot hear
I tell you this as a story
Go then for the victory,
I have seen a friend wail
Myself, I had then, to fail
Because nothing was useful
Everything appeared wasteful
Put in more and lose more
Forget it and have a sore,
The earth is a big boil
It has not a good soil
Tortured and wearied, we are
Stripped naked, everything is bare
But life has nothing to lose
Rather we suffer in the nose
I write my name on the wall
They push me around the hall
Up and down I feel annoyance
In and out I seek vengeance
I pray against any delay
Yet my message has no relay,
Crying, I shout Alas!

I go for my geography atlas
To help me get some map
Where there is more gap,
So that I can go to God
And plead with Him for a nod
Going there is not easy
Trying it keeps you busy,
Any friend takes a shield
He does not want to yield
Men are near to deceive
Angels far to receive,
Hurrying to them takes energy
It may need long liturgy
I do not know botany
But I know some litany,
Let one go for the other
Until we appreciate another
Lie down on the rug
Hold a water filled mug
Let nobody stop my good
Because they use me as wood,
Though this trouble I fight
And darkness turns to light
I have many things to assume
Even with some very nice perfume,
My troubles push me to the edge
This ridicules my little knowledge
It exposes my ignorance
Leaving me a light assurance,
Nobody can always comprehend
Especially when they pretend
Show them the right track
They give you their back,
My name is not Clinton

But I have some good cotton,
Another name for the mild
If he is not a growing child
Walk down the darkness
You will be in the wilderness,
Some people sell their gold
Because they feel cold.

CHAPTER 17:
TOMORROW COUNTS

If it is hard to eat today
It may be easy to walk away
Starting any type of relationship
Without true fellowship
Is like building a mansion
Beneath the high tension,
Anybody coming out of teen
Looks good and green
But some want to look black
So they enter into a big sack
This gets them tied up
Some, their blood fill the cup.
Again, be careful to connect
And make your choices, correct
Otherwise, anything you sow in heap
From there you have to reap
The rains will be abundant
But the harvest may be unpleasant
Inside your bone marrow
Writes joy and sorrow
Follow those that are upright
If you want to be bright
People run around for money
But the wise go for real honey,
Which gives happiness
And less sadness
Bone to bone, you live
Flesh to flesh, we give.
When I seat on the bench
I always have to drench
But lo, there is fire

Sure it is my only desire
As I go up to the mountain
I discover there is a fountain
Do not relent I hear again
My voice is clear and plain
Never commit murder
But always use the ladder
I will set with you on the table,
Be very approachable
There are things to teach
They are not within reach
So learn like the ant
Be big like the elephant,
Your life can be exemplary
If you know it is temporary
Now, stand to your feet
Take the best you meet,
Consider the better you see
Doubt the good for a fee
The world sets you on motion
Dictating your pace and emotion
Try out every incident
Even if it is by accident,
I warn you now be wise
There are falls as you rise
Eating g from a golden plate
Would not write on your slate
Sure, it will remain blank
Whether or not you have a bank,
Sometime I fall on the tile
And tear some good file
It is very monstrous
Deadly, evil and disastrous
If I had gone to 'Athen'

Maybe would have lost then
Many people enjoy tragedy
Others go for just comedy
The song we all sing
Is to have a nice king
But this has been delayed
And many have not stayed.

CHAPTER 18:
SABOTAGE KILLS

Shooting ourself on the leg
Leaves us to beg,
I went to the market
Only could I buy a bucket,
Life is more than we know
Fact is bigger than we show
Studying has made us wild
Not even a kid is now mild,
We cause havoc instead of knowledge
And also burn the college
If you know more loneliness
You will value Godliness.
Our world filled with immorality
Has a brother called brutality
Try your best to be fair
They will brand you unfair,
There is a notorious band
They have ugly stand
Attempt to be a hero
Then, they bring you to zero
Associating with a witch
Means entering some ditch.
I know someone as Richard
But he has no orchard
His struggle is to have a kid
That he may get to the mid,
If you have planted a flower
It surely needs some shower,
If you dig a pit
You may not sit,
Wherever you live and work

There you take your stock
Do not give an account
Also hide the real amount,
Someday you will be called
And your evidence walled
The sin of a good man
Is likely to be spread by the fan,
The cloth we wear hides a lot
They tell just little or not
But on our finger is a ring
It does not give us a wing
Yet we want by all means to fly
Especially seeing the best on the sky
It is not a kid that wears pant
Because some elders are like infant
They neither grow nor change
Just far from the range,
People want to live in the stratosphere
When the world is losing the atmosphere
I wonder what they want
When they need to be vigilant,
Somebody wrote an article
In it he drew some particle
He is not even an artist
Neither is he a scientist
But because he is talking
He has to keep walking,
Afraid of the mob, too close
We have to find another repose
An angry mind is a beast
It is like having an ugly feast
Run away from him
He sings devilish hymn,
The building is on fire

Do not sink in the mire
Make it now very important
If you really want to be a giant,
Think of what is coming
Forget about the one going
Let there be a birth
And a worthy rebirth.

CHAPTER 19:
KEEP FAITH

Tie yourself on a wrapper
Do not be a bad rapper,
I warn you never be a racist
Also do not be a rapist
Life has a lot to pay
It may even be a day
Our blessing came last
But it made us leave the past,
Do not go for any treasure
That has little or no measure
There are things of advantage
They take you out of bondage,
Relax, life will be good soon
It will be beautiful like the moon
Evil will be no more
Just like now or before,
Dance, the future is bright
Rejoice, there is green light
I have wondered the season
Now I know the reason,
Rise up, make a noise
Have your neighbour to poise
Go out for leisure
Let nothing be a seizure,
That line is now breaking
The foundation is shaking
The world is rendering apart
Bear this in your heart
Tell all to get set
Let them gather their pet
For everything is going home

Where our king has to come
Drop the gun, sheath the sword
There is a long strong chord
It is coming to tie everybody
The one holding it is somebody,
There is nothing to squeeze
Because we have a gentle breeze
Travel also to Alaska
Be there in Madagascar,
One thing is sure here
It is neither here nor there
Life will end somewhere cool
Soft and mild like the wool
Touch the hen, feel the bull
Everything on the full,
I tell you visit a country
Also live in the monastery,
On my way to Sydney
I must not sell my kidney,
I need to mark my utensil
Though I have no pencil
If you read my biography
You still need some geography
Know the earth and her shape
Also plant some grape,
Around the globe and universe
We have just an auto reverse
Gather it with a rake
At least for your own sake
If something must erupt
Let same not be corrupt
There is somewhere a burden
Let us wait and deaden
Otherwise rushing, we spoil

Though we work and toil,
Love may not be by Jack
So it can still suffer lack
Give as free as air
Make it many like hair
Choose for yourself alone
For none to break your bone.

CHAPTER 20:
PUSH

At the face of regret
They may pull you like magnet
Turning you round the clock
You may hit on the rock,
Grow instead like a tree
From everything be free
If you are a woman
Be not after woe unto man
I learnt some small trick
So I can no more be sick
Because already I am tired
And this gets me inspired
My work is on the stage
Whether or not I earn any wage
Pull down the ancient city
Let us learn now simplicity,
Terrifying is the old pattern
Here is a shinning lantern
Rise up and carry your cross
Wake, you are your own boss
If you borrow you must repay
This I told you from the first day
Teach your children to obey law
Tell them to forget the flaw,
My people want to perish
But I want them to flourish
Life is rich and gainful
It is empty too and painful
If you want to eat the barley
Also go down to the valley
My coach has been stained

But I want it retained
All the people who are young
Sometimes do right or wrong,
The elders have learnt much
This makes them sell their lunch
Nobody at all is appreciative
Even for getting something lucrative
Let us take some oat
For us to row the boat
Whether or not we have a telephone
We still need some mobile phone,
Otherwise life will send us far
Where there would be a bar
Then none could get across
To at least one out of a gross
Our friends live in the cave
So we must extend the wave.

CHAPTER 21:
IRONY

There is someone in the city
On the villagers, he does not pity,
To decorate and plant flower
Is not harder than building a tower
A man was made a chief
Even when he is a cruel thief,
Granted, nobody is perfect
But none should be a subject
The world we live is bending
We should help it in blending
Ugly men tie a long rope
For others who could not cope,
Tell them to position well
You become the next tree they fell
The issue is not with yesterday
Rather it is now and today
We have refused to repent
And have chosen to relent
Troubles give no one credit
Instead they feed all with debit
Children know not what happened
Even when their eyes are sharpened,
They can play with the leper
As if they are holding paper
Get any issue complicated
You must be implicated
In a coat of many colours
All would seem just ridiculous
I know of a great wonder
This we all must ponder
But amazingly it is neglected

Even when it should be selected,
Listen, let us save the world
And stop planting any discord
If you own a big farm
Hold it fine and firm
Because life itself is weak
Even those at the peak,
We have made a mistake
So all have to partake
Nobody is exempted
Whether or not you are prompted
My mother has not been to Rome
So she is always at home,
Never forget what you go through
People die several times a day
Yet none earns their pay
Some fight to weigh you down
They want you always to frown,
But they will only succeed
When you allow them feed
A determined man can win
It does not matter his sin
Anger can make you fall
And look terribly small
Pride can take you to a tower
And crush you like a world power
Ignorance can dig your grave
And make you appear less brave
I warn you be careful
If you wish to be fruitful,
Some started and ended
Some never, but pretended
It is not good to be flat
Instead better, being fat,

Friends like enemies can kill
They can make you stand still,
Then you would be lifeless
And they would share your dress
Caring less about anything
They have achieved something

CHAPTER 22:
TOO UNFAIR

Yes, they killed their friend
At a very bad and crooked end
I tell you brothers are dangerous
Sisters too are very cancerous
Mind one forget the other
Love all and one another,
At last you will wail
For you must then fail
Because their aim is ugly
So they have to bully,
Discuss inside with a voice
That night they eat your rice
Nothing is there to change
They will leak you like orange,
Forget the voices you hear
They only can create fear
Give them the least attention
You will remain in tension
Men are evil and wicked
So their ways are crooked
Anything you have to smuggle
Let it not be a struggle,
For life is not predictable
But we can make it comfortable,
Those who went to school
Sometimes forget their tool
When they fail to push
They cannot often flush
Look at a mere crayon
It can paint a dragon
Not all about eating fish

We must not remain selfish
Nobody comes like a giant
All enters like an ant
But the hero is made
And the crown fits his head
If you should be a thinker
Then always refill your the tanker,
Even if you carry only petrol
Let nothing loosen your control
Sometimes we become a toad
To help us cross the road,
It does not end there
If we are still nowhere
So, arise and shine
Anywhere even in the shrine
At peace, we lose freedom
Bound, we experience boredom.

CHAPTER 23:
IMAGINE

They stole my book
To pay their cook
I will watch and see
They all must flee,
It delays the promise
As it leads to demise
Let there be a remission
We need no permission,
People have suffered enough
The road has been rough
If you are a freeholder
You also are a leaseholder
Because life is magic
Full of everything tragic,
Look far in the east
You will back the west
Move down the south
You will be far from the north,
I told you if you need a seat
Drop the band and never beat
I know someone, cripple
Who has touched many people,
He must not preach sermon
Before he can cast out any demon
Your life is an episode
Whether or not you can explode
Be warned, it is horrible
The world is just terrible
If you believe you are wise
It can help you fast to rise,
But remember it is not all

There is an answer to every call,
Think about the past
Let it not be too fast,
You must learn a big deal
A better way to easily heal
Lightning comes with the rain
Thunder can bring along pain,
The way you can always cherish
Is that which allows you flourish
Do not love that which is bad
Lest you make your generation sad
Wanting to live well and long
Allow God to make you strong,
Troubles abound since yesterday
But let us await the coming day
Anger can foil your power
And wither you like a flower.

CHAPTER 24:
SHUN PRIDE

Arrogance can dwindle your zeal
And you lose out a good meal
During the trade of barter
None knew money would come,
 some gave out their donkey
Just for a little monkey
To lose big and grief
 lack want, long,
Making vital decisions in a haste
Can make one lose his taste,
Now and again be careful
Make your life very meaningful
Servants are taken for granted
Those who are not, never granted
Some people are better off
Whereas some are in handcuff
Let nothing get you amazed
Because it too, can be erased
Those who do not make their bed
Sometimes are poorly fed,
If you have gone to prison
You may have no comparison
Refresh those who are tired
Never let them get fired,
Up and down, we all toss
Back and front, life is the boss
We need not to resign
But much to redesign
There is a big definition
It requires our recognition
A lot has been proposed

They were naturally opposed,
Dancing in the synagogue
Is not lying in the morgue
No man knows best life
When there is no wife,
Favour can go extra mile
Labour can stand for awhile
My mission is provide
And not to divide
Let us go for an order
As we fight all disorder,
The life we love and respect
Can make us not to disrespect
Sow some tiny seed
Make sure you weed,
It matters too the plant
And the harvest you want,
You will eat the bread
As far as you can spread,
I have a beautiful rug
It gives warm hug,
I love to pray and wait
Even when I go to plait
As a lady and a single
It may be hard to mingle,
For the man, searching
He is readily marching
There is a time to weep
It may be when to sweep,
Around us is a great river
It causes drowning, however
Fighting to save your throat
May strip off your coat
When the water is on your neck

You can never go for a peck
If you are wearing a short
You may swim to the port,
Sometimes, there is smoke
The day troubles awoke,
Nobody defends the island
Assuming we have one hand.

CHAPTER 25:
OPEN UP

If you are a miser
You may get no wiser
Hiding your gift is stupid
No matter the guise or bid,
Our talents someday intercede
 When we are just to concede
By the way, we need to pull
For we must get to the full
Never be stopped from hoping
Unless you want to be losing,
Seeing one who is dangerous
Does not tell one to be monstrous
The world is a big grave
We can still help and save,
Trouble not your neighbour
Scatter not his labour
If you want to grow big
Turn nobody into pig,
It is normal and real
Lest you bear destructive seal
Let your work give you rest
And have a positive interest,
Men who die will live again
But let it be not in vain
We need not be a river
Before we can be a giver
The little we have can go far
And shine brighter like a star,
The big time on the wall
Ticks always even during fall
If you are a good hammer

You can be used in summer
I do not need a black coat
If I can only look like a goat,
I want that of many colours
To add to other lives, flavours
I am from the eastward
I pray always to go forward
There are many traveling abroad
We must welcome them aboard
 For our journey to be smooth
A succour we must sooth,
Those who are too silent
We must help not to be latent
Our creed we must recite
Even if we are still in the site,
Let these words enter your ears
Eat it like the meat of mother bears.

CHAPTER 26:
PRAY ALWAYS

Prayer is a wonderful key
It is stronger than whisky
Drink it and grow stronger
Use it and look younger,
Disturb the gates of hell
Bind the demons in cell,
Lock up their gate
And leave them to fate
Look away from greed
If you want to proceed,
I say it again, another time
It is not in anyway a crime
Let there be love and unity
Cleanse your hands in purity,
Deceive yourself not God
He holds a correcting rod
The world is too hilly
It can name you even Billy,
Once you come late
You may lose an estate
If you desire that victory
Just make it a history
Thinking of it is a wish
Eating it is already a dish,
Let us be a champion
Rather than being a scorpion
We have something too precious
It may not be that delicious
But if we accurately play our card
Our winning will be sure and hard,
All we do, just like any game

Has a making and a frame,
It is never a contradiction
Rather a strong prediction
Whoever uses the wall clock
May not escape they that mock,
Watch the rotation of the fan
It moves not like the van
Some men bear the name Robert
Others bear the like, Norbert,
They may be from different places
They all have many faces,
Life has something in common
And a particular courage to summon,
Any who fears will crash
Even without a single clash
Let your boldness be like stone
Though soft be your bone,

CHAPTER 27:
BE UNIQUE

In any chosen group or class
Someone must break the glass
Let there be a better stitch
Consider also a loud pitch,
If there is no frequency
Bear every consequency
Wearing a cap is normal
Making noise, like animal
Selecting the right gear
Tends to reduce the fear,
But jumping a high wall
Teaches one no basket ball
Black and white, red and yellow
None makes one a fellow,
Among everything we read
On top is the lead
The day we leave the park
It will make a positive mark,
Let us listen as we wrestle
Lest we hear not the whistle
Put on all your jeans
They can never give you beans,
Sing the song of redemption
If you do not build on assumption
Wear off your clean shirt
Turn it not into skirt
Men who die are not living
And they can never be giving
See an angel descending from above
He is flying like a dove,
For those who write with ink

They also paint in pink
The sun is like a light
It gives a great sight,
Just like the full moon
That makes the dark like noon,
Any car with wiper
Blows like the piper
As attractive as the rainbow
Bending too like the elbow,
For the man named Paul
He may neither run nor crawl
He is not a strong member
Just an ordinary number
There is something about camera
It does not solve algebra
Going by some regression
None makes any progression.

CHAPTER 28:
NOT BY POWER

If you have some lump
Do not cool or slump,
It can kill or frustrate
This you can illustrate
Receive the good idea
Spread it on the media,
Go to the sea or beach
There is nobody to impeach,
Around the opening or leakage
We can install some storage
So that we may not lose much
We can take our brunch
If we rise above hate,
Then we would open the gate
This is a fight we must win
Let it cost us every pin
Dwelling in terror will be gone
Living in unity will be done,
The only thing we are to follow
Is that which has no sorrow
Take me round the universe
And also make a reverse
For me to make a conclusion
I hope this is not an illusion,
My friend is called Joe
We wish not to make a foe,
His younger brother is Peter
He drinks excess water
Both love Margaret
I warn them to avoid regret,
There is a ladder we must step

It will be of great help
In order not to contact bacteria
We must not run away from the criteria,
The robbers on parade
They are ready to be made
Nobody can tell their plan
But we know they have a clan,
Their leader is not a ghost
They have mounted their post,
I brought out my palm
Showing that I am calm
Believing to be seen well
Taking the place of a model,
Warriors give us the secret
They make it very concrete
Yet the more we come near
The least we could hear.

CHAPTER 29:
THE MORE YOU LOOK THE LESS YOU SEE

My dream is to be perfect
Never to be a suspect
Because I am like a magnet
Attracting all to the banquet,
The best game is not to steal
Rather to be good and real
I have a great team
Our mindset is to conquer
With the help of our maker,
The land we own and cultivate
Has much for us to incubate
I tell you, have a good motive
Then your zeal will be active
Lie flat like a lice
Bid it like some price,
Sometimes leaving your lane
May result to going insane
Once in awhile you move mad
Life is like a jungle
But wear it like a bangle,
When we have nothing to eat
We still can achieve a feat
My purpose is what I know
The reason I do not show
Many take me for a fool
Because I play so cool
I bet I must fly
As far as the sky
A covenant made by God
Nothing breaks it, not even a rod
A good name is written on the sky

There, lies and blackmails cannot fly
Let hatred and jealousy build a ladder
Let envy and wickedness commit murder
Let gossip and conspiracy surround the table
God is neither blind nor cheatable,
Surely, wasted is the time spent in mockery
Regrettable, the passion burned in treachery,
I know of Campbell
She is not a rebel.
My president Goodluck
Was wished badluck.
Go to Doctor Patrick
He will help you pick.
If the land is nasty
Then we make it tasty,
In the country of Poland
One can bear Roland
In the east of Mexico
They do dance disco
All over Europe
They use microscope
Because it is an aid
You can be paid,
If you can produce it
And make it very fit,
People use what they like
Not that of the man, Mike
I have this message to convey
It does not need a survey
Worry not, life is beautiful
If we agree to make it fruitful
My wish is not to derail
Instead for us to prevail,
The moment we fight

We lose our power and might
Then gathering would be by force
And we disfigure our horse
We may not fight any beast
But God can reduce it to the least.

CHAPTER 30:
WONDER
People who are undercover
Hardly can have a true lover
Because they work as agents
They will never be reagents,
I have tried all about tolerance
Playing cool for ignorance
Yet certain things fight me
And cut off my whole knee
Failing is not the point
Rather having a disjoint,
Managing to hold on along
Can cause one to get it wrong,
Sure, we need to be fair
So that we can as well pair,
Being wicked gets us no good
Instead it ruins our neighbourhood
The way we are is natural
And we have made it cultural,
Look up the sky for a second
You can draw out a pond
It may not be too sudden
Provided you are not harden,
What we all can tell
May not sound very well.
A very clean bed
Needs not a bloodshed
In the field of battle
They can kill even a cattle
We need some argumentation
To avoid great lamentation
Listen to those who overcame
They had tortured frame,

See it with your eyes again
And do not think of being just fain.
Living inside a good batcher
Can make you too a butcher
But life is not steady
So let us always be ready,
My hands cross my shoulder
And I try not to be colder
Relieved, I try to assume
Take away pain and stress
Then forget the whole mess
Learning is a way of life
Inside and outside the strife
Forget what they will say
Make sure you have a stay.

CHAPTER 31:
DEEPER

I know not the sound
But I know it is around
It looms by the corner
Speeding like a great runner,
The one finishing a marathon
Occupying the forest like python.
If you want to be a priest
Then never be a beast
It is one thing to be a goddess
Another to be a princess
I have seen many decay
As they wish to replay,
Life may not have another chance
Though we wallow in ignorance
Let us renew our knowledge
That will give us more courage,
Otherwise we end like them
Whether or not at the helm,
Growing up is an edge
Going down can be a hedge
The last can get a gift
But it may not be swift
I warn you again be alert
Keep not your energy inert,
They taught us about kinetic
They did not forget the magnetic
Whatever can surround the pole
It may not bear any hole
Let us take this into consideration
In case we are learning mensuration
If you have nothing to defend

Then you may never attend
Unless you are a spirit
Who needs nothing like affidavit
Look, beside is a game
It brings anyone to fame,
Talking is not a reason
For it may be out of season
There is a thing of joy
Everybody here can enjoy
What it tells is reasonable
The story is understandable
When we get to the lake
We shall mind our brake
Because it will wash us clean
All whether fat or lean
Nothing on earth is hidden
Including those overridden,
Some moment a go we were fine
Now I can hardly imagine
Why everything went poor
And closed the widest door
Tomorrow is looking good
But today there is no food,
Unbelievable it seems to all
Tossing it is like a ball,
Life is not a venture
Rather a big adventure
Knowing this is the key
And being smart like the monkey,
As we grow we forget a lot
It does not mean we are harlot
There and here we can sleep
Now and then we may weep,
Yes, nothing makes one happy

Because life then is snappy
Abundantly it can rain
Rarely it may retain
Close the gap, buckle up
Focus, look at the top
If you fall, you become the foot mat
But if you stand, you grow fat.

CHAPTER 32:
CHANGE

In the land of the blind
Someone can renew their mind
Instead of remaining the name
Work on cleaning your name,
It speaks when we are far
When we have crossed the bar
Foreigners hear and learn it
Even those in the pit,
Do not be a load or bag
Containing a kind of rag
If you can crush the wall
Please have light to install
Those who build a bridge on land
They are shallow like the sand
You can build the highest tower
But nonsense without a shower
Diseases invade us like enemy
They form nothing but no remedy
Who cares what we become?
Whether we all die or some
I warn again be on the guard
You do not need a bodyguard,
Death can scatter a life jacket
It too can spare a mere basket
Let nothing trouble your heart
They win when you lose the art,
Believe the word I tell you now
Never you ask questions or how
A letter above the sky
Asks the question, why?
But nothing can stop the lame

If he does not like shame
Three times I make this remark
I do not mean to bark,
Listen and be glad
Let nothing make you sad
The end is near us
May we never lose focus
Each day we pray and sing
Waiting for what it will bring,
Every time we watch and meditate
Looking unto our saviour to imitate
Amazingly we suffer a heartbreak
This parts us like a shipwreck
Those who know not do not understand
Even when the grieved chop off their hand,
Beside living there is dying
Near losing there is trying
I have died and awoke
Now I cannot again choke
Hatred has made me a thief
Wickedness also made me chief
Evil men because of me, went hunting
My poor spirit they kept taunting,
They saw nobody around me
So they clouded me like bee,
Though we will keep escaping
God will stop them from raping,
Let the world bear me witness
I did not disturb their quietness
About this time they retreat
Forging ahead for my meat
They want my blood and flesh
They long for it to be fresh,
We all will reap what we sow

Including the blood we made to flow
Plus the ones we drink
Because they were too weak,
God knows the height and peak
Nobody will escape His judgement
It does not depend on movement.

CHAPTER 33:
KNOW THIS

Our world is like a camp
It will be dark without lamp
Hide your light and be in darkness
Use it and remain in boldness
Let the children sing us a song
Make it not short but long
Then we would hear the voice of God
It will be on the lowest chord,
My friend has some talent
He leases it for rent
Being happy how it goes
Not believing he has some foes
One day, normal everything seems
Unfortunately his head he redeems
I warn you life is not full
Do not fight it like a bull
Consider the trouble we face
We must not allow this pace
My fear is that big torture
Which in our heart we nurture
Someday it may sprout
And everything will fall apart
Hear this all over again
This earth now is not plain,
Our prayer is not slow
We will make it a blow
Else we may keep retaining
And our values get discarding
People who are not humble
At a point they all wobble,
I made up my mind to pass

If not the door is strong brass
It was harder than any other
Looking down on even any mother
My sister won a jack pot
But nothing in it she got,
They stole it away immediately
Even when she knew it intimately
I wonder what would be better
Especially in the years latter
Some people play golf
And others become wolf
Meanwhile, some know the reality
They just want to make it vanity,
My friend is called Solomon
He likes a lot of lemon
After falling down the tree
He had no option than to flee
Anything you love can kill
If you like getting your fill,
My partner is a dreamer
He is always much warmer.
You can build an ark
Just to get his remark
I passionately hate disappointment
Mostly from the part of government,
But my God has done it for me
He did it when prayer scarred my knee
We made it our passion
Achieving it like a mission
Suddenly He got me shattered
Since then, yet to be gathered
This world is a danger zone
I laugh at those who make it clone
Do not touch the trigger

It can serve as ginger
If you are a superstar
You need not be a gangster
This can ruin your face
And make you lose your place
People get it negative
And refuse the positive.

CHAPTER 34:
IT DOES MATTER

We bought a new born puppy
A better place for it is the lobby
We thought it could survive alone
So we left it on its own,
A few days later, it died
Forgetting it was harder but we tried
We learnt that we need each
 Even when we go to the beach
Outside, we are too good
But inside, we keep mood
Because we condemn wrongly
And believe it so strongly
Let nature teach us well
Let it have our issues to dispel
We are things God will not forbid
Rather He will make them solid,
A saint named Cyril
Also saw a lot of peril
These days it is not so
 For they would rather not go
If the suffering is much or severe
Better for them to be servants mere
If you love your life any day
You will lose it at last, someday
Anybody can be a queen
Even without being keen
She can choose to be Jezebel
After bearing the name Annabel
No lane without an obstacle
But there can be on it a miracle
The things we love and procure

Can cause us to endure
If we focus on sentiment
Let us therefore show gratitude
And also at the right magnitude
Things that make us proud
Are not written on the cloud
We bear them in our body
As we sing a good melody
The lantern we produce
Must be good to use
So that we do not stagger
And burst into anger
Forward in the light
Strong for the fight,
Ready against any circumstance
Adapt to future resistance.

CHAPTER 35:
LET GO

The wonders we seek like gold
They too can keep the future on hold,
Trouble yourself against no man
Unless the war has finally began
I have warned you to pray
So that you do not stray
There is a hand wanting to shield
All those who are in the field
But it must be invited
For it to be very committed
In the midst of the storm
It can protect even the worm
This is nothing but the greatest
Because it can wait till the latest
Arise and begin the search
Let it become also a research
If you make yourself a candidate
You can never forget your date
There is a friend, very dear
He can never eat your pear
Flogging may not be the best
But helping can do the rest,
Gossiping is very destructive
It has never been protective,
Those who ask for supply
Must first apply
It is with their demand
They will fill their hand,
But for one to be a leader
He must also be a reader
For him to understand

When, how to command,
The wishes we all make
Are not only for our sake
It must spread all over
For us to be a world mover
There is a man called Duke
His friend is named Luke
Both married a woman
Already engaged to a man
It led to divorce
Which they did by force,
The issue was very bitter
But they can make it better
Love is not a fool
We swim in it as a pool
It has done a lot of work
And much more in stock.

CHAPTER 36:
ALL IS NOT GOLD

Planting inside, a silicon
May alter your skeleton
Even if on the contrary
You can ask Doctor Hillary
Stay away from any hazard
Though it includes lizard,
We have a big reproach
It is not only the coach,
This is a united team
Tighten each, every beam
If we decide to separate
We cannot fabricate
Look up and see a future
Think back, imagine a posture
Failing to achieve victory
Could de a bad history,
My father is not an Engineer
But I know him as a pioneer,
He is not in the government
But he manns his regiment.
Your name can be Patrick
Yet you cannot lay a brick
There was not a lunatic
Who entered the titanic,
Falling is the nature of man
Even those who lifted the ban
A time comes to fade
Including those that are made
On the ocean shore
The cold is much more
So with the wind and tide

It may be difficult to guide
Nobody can dream of a mob
Including they that hit the club
If we can learn cleanliness
Then we can practice Godliness
Nothing good makes sense
When done in pretense
Some people eat vulture
Making it their culture,
There is an old bishop
He has a big shop
Also ordinary, a deacon
Who sells nothing but beacon
They all have a union
Calling people for communion
Gathering people for congregation
Preaching against segregation,
Their friend is a reverend
He helps them comprehend
There is also a catechist
Partaking in the Eucharist
The body is in love
Focusing all above
Another in their midst is a Dutch
He uses a costly golden watch
But people do not cross the border
As long as he does not murder
Many know he is a visitor
Yet they hide their resistor
Because in the world of greed
Nothing can be a good deed,
I say it again be casual
Do everything as usual
Bearing in your mind heaven

And removing even the little leaven
Children who do not listen to elders
May not make good welders
Wisdom is for us to institute
Not for any to prostitute
Anyone who is a coward
Easily can lose his reward.

CHAPTER 37:
GOOD TO GO

It is good to be ambitious
And not being superstitious
Better for us to be eager
As we pray to grow bigger
Wait for your own turn
If you really want to return,
Do not at all be envious
Watch and not be jealous,
All these can destroy
No matter who you employ
The pope lives in Rome
There permanently is his home
Outside, he has forgotten
Because it is unfair and rotten,
If you travel to Mecca
You may not see Rebecca
Liking her may be good
But she cannot leave motherhood
A lot of troubles keep us asking
They make life much tasking
It does not stop the best
Though we live in a nest
Telling a story is not bad
Because it can make us glad,
What matters is the end
If we can make amend
Seeing all in the television
And having all in provision
Dreaming well in the night
And getting them all right,
Praying straight and hoping same

All these can help us tame
Loving only your profession
Making the night confession,
Writing well the law
Finely can serve as a straw
There is only one birth
Sure, there is too, death
If the world can make us free
Then we will never again see
Life is a journey of torture
With no regards to your stature
The road is hilly and mountainous
All round is very religious
So far we are lost and tired
Looking like it was conspired,
The closer we become, the more fearful
The wider we are, the more needful
There is a need for spoon
But stupid inside a lagoon,
As friendly as the dolphin
But not when in a coffin
You can hide in the pot
When you hear a gunshot
Nothing stops you from hiding
Though you are falling or sliding,
My wish is never to fail
Instead to feel that I am frail
I started this in September
Hoping to be done by October
This is an ordinary target
Sure, it worries me to get
Because ahead is a treasure
Which nobody can measure
I have something to decide

Though there I do not reside,
After lifting the arrow
At flight is the sparrow
It means I can fight
For putting an enemy to flight,
Many people are not aware
So they do not mind or care.

CHAPTER 38:
YES

Never have I been to Alaska
Only heard of Madagascar
My country is Nigeria
It far from Algeria
I am from Africa
But must visit America
Hearing about the horoscope
I love Europe,
My strength is in the Bible
Let it be written on the marble,
For them, us and the unborn
It can feed us like the corn
Come back from New York
You must use the fork
If you drink from that well,
I love Mary Slessor
She does not have a successor,
It looks like a fairy tale
Listening about Florence Nightingale
The then war in Biafra
Was a great cobra
It claimed great and small
But it stood up very tall.
People who are very rascal
They can party in blackmail
Just for something to nail
Others who long for craftiness
May even abound in emptiness
Yet these things are core
They all had something before
In the bid to stand alone

They made, their own throne,
Unfortunately they die young
Sometimes like a wooden gong
It is not when they stop breathing
But when they are wrongly breeding
Show yourself the true way
This is not a calculated play
Someday life would be gone
All will be alone with none
Then everything will be true
Binding each like a glue
Now is the time a chance
Let us learn well the dance
At the end, there is no back
Everything will seem to be black,
There is a Man who is fair
He is not Tony Blair
We can never bear his name
Nor attempt his frame
Many think it is a fairy tale
Because they look pale,
Someday death visits the surgeon
And all things even the pigeon
We have had enough practicals
Witnesses are the chemicals
Aloof and astray we went
Scattered, destroyed and bent
Yes, gather all for judgement,
This is not for procurement
Long a go we lost it all
Before time, there was a fall
But thank God there came a saviour
He became a big reservoir,
Except Him it would have been hopeless

With Him, it is just blessedness,
People claim what they are not
Hot for cold and cold for hot
On their own they are good
But it is a big falsehood,
They can kill if you resist
So nobody tries to insist
This they do in operation
Now they get cooperation
Killing is the order of the day
The society is in big decay,
Conspiracy hooks them in the neck
Yet they care not to check
Greed gives them a kiss
And they live in bliss,
Lust has got them arrested
And they enjoy being molested,
Fear encamped their image
So they closed the new page
Indiscipline stole their manhood
Forcing out of way the brotherhood,
Indecency locked them in a yard
And murdered coldly their guard
Lies blindfolded their eyes
Contaminated and destroyed their sacrifice
Bribery killed their conscience
Corruption scattered their foundation
Eating deep the corners of the nation.

CHAPTER 39:
A CRAZY WORLD

Inside this terrible boat
All drenched wearing a coat
But we know we are strong
Just that something is wrong
Up there they sing some chorus
Down here we are porous,
Take it to heart or not
Something is inside the pot
Care less or much I am sure
That this life is never secure
The elders drink blood
It overwhelms like flood,
If you are for harmony
They put you in agony
If you have a better thought
Sure, you must be fought,
Young people have sold their ear
And this is terrible to bear
If nothing is being done
Then this world is gone,
I wonder about the unborn
What will be of their horn
A polluted seed
Hardly can make good breed,
Very close is the vampire
He is taking over the empire
Having the looks of a conqueror
He is worshipped like an emperor,
He devours like a beast
Not minding the least
Across the border is his toast

He has enlarged his coast
Forcing some people to sleep
Flogging some others to weep,
Many are in his hot ring
He is now their only king
Give us peace once again
Take away all this pain
Fight with even the cattle
You can never lose a battle,
Give us great victory
Even in this enemy territory
Cause us to raise your banner
And enjoy another lord's dinner,
Burn up the red flag
And give us the green tag
Let this war be finished
And your kingdom established.

CHAPTER 40:
ARISE O LORD

This world is your vine
Therefore make it very fine
But if you delay more
The devil will get to the core,
Wear all thy strength
Redress the world at length
Cut off all that is bad
Let none again be sad,
Those who cannot preach
Let them learn to teach
Far and near people are bound
Search and let all be found
Lord this world is tiring
Everybody is just boring,
Those you trust make you cry
The ones you love just fry,
Leave it to forge ahead
You can never be made
Grab it and deal with it
You hardly can be fit,
If you give in to anger
You remain like a hanger
For troubles shooting from the breast
Seldom; give anyone any rest
Watch closely you see a hand
It may be buried in the sand
Strictly it is from within
The most difficult to win,
It is there in your closet
Not everywhere on this planet
As you fight to rekindle

The job is to make you dwindle

CHAPTER 41:
STAND TALL

If your spirit is bold
Then you may not fold
Otherwise, you may be forgotten
Whether or not you are begotten,
Never you at all do evil
I still bet, nearer is the devil
Fight everything not to faint
Nobody will ever make you a saint
If you should be glorified
Sure, they must have you crucified
They bind your knowledge
Especially if you are from college
Their fierce anger makes you afraid
They can only make you a maid,
Tell the truth and be dead
So that they can raise their head
Bring up some good point
They bring a disjoint
 Lord there is a lot to do
 Please never you say no.
Girls wear their mothers' pant
And walk like an elephant,
Boys sleep in their fathers' room
And become the bridegroom
When you come somehow close
They burn and bury your nose
When you pray for restoration

You become an abomination,
Around you, they hold a knife
Clearly saying they steal your life
They will reduce you to zero
If you prove to be a hero
When I look around and behind
Only fear grips my mind,
If you stand up tall
They force you to fall
If you keep too busy
They make it uneasy
If you go away hiding
They announce a bad tiding
If there is a God up there
If He is near and everywhere
Please this is a distress call
Break open this thick wall
I have a case to be addressed
I pray let it be redressed
Brood over this crazy world
This is my earnest prayer, lord.

CHAPTER 42:
BE CAREFUL

Declare the greatest zeal
They gather and put a seal.
Tell them your dream
They destroy your team.
Wearing a hard shell like tortoise
But a big enemy in disguise,
Physically he looks like a lover
Generally he is agent undercover.
So those things he cannot afford
Which are in your record
Keep him so much troubled
Until he has them dismantled.
Fear your friend, avoid your foe
If possible walk and tiptoe
Just eat well it will sink
Never force it with bad drink
Otherwise it will be a mess
Giving you terror and stress,
This world is deeply crazy
Due to that, some are lazy
They have vowed to be idle
Not even picking a needle
This baffles those who run
As they hear firing of gun,
Come back home to relax
You must pay your tax
Press your shirt and look good
Not within the brotherhood,
Because your head is not big
And your buttocks dirty like pig
You waste your precious time

If you cannot commit crime.

CHAPTER 43:
REFLECTION

Lord, hide not your face
You are losing the human race
It is never in your nature
To support any bad culture
So hesitate not, to act
Let your people be intact,
If you are a living water
Let your people be no dead matter
Keep this world lively afloat
Let it not be a scape goat
Holy spirit, if you were a police
You would never kill a novice,
Jesus if you were a soldier
You would never war your brother
God if you were an elderly
You would never act wickedly,
Heaven, if you were on earth
We would have not known death
As we pray more for freedom
Deeper we swim in boredom,
Wear a fine linen purple
Beautify it as a couple
Tomorrow it is gone completely
And you cannot mourn it secretly,
They want to hear you cough
But hate to hear you laugh
Keep a thousand miles from fire

But stay half a mile to your desire,
If you are the only judge
Do not harbour any grudge
Hold unto that which is right
Though they put up a fight,
Life is not all about living
A part of it is just giving
Some give out their conscience
Others teach the real science,
The fool revolves round it
The wise uses it to sit
Let us stop pretending
This world is soon ending,
Cut your coat to your cloth
Far from the truth,
There is a portable majority
There is a great minority,
If you have the courage
You will never be below average
They will force you to win
But inscribe your head on the coin,
So even if you die later
Your name will be known after
If you have a mail to deliver
Kindly give it to a believer
For it will never make sense
To anyone sitting on the fence
Cook some rich sweet soup
It can only serve some group,
Put a star inside a cage
Someday it mounts the stage
Some people are there to salute
While some are near to pollute,
Tell them to do some good

They will serve you as food,
Wake up, it is sunrise
Let your heart be wise.

CHAPTER 44:
WATCH

Around us, there is a smoke
We are beginning to choke
Alas, put off the fire
Let us cut totally the wire,
Examine yourself and know
How best this world can grow
Crush the story rock
Open that hard lock,
Throw always those sticks
Lay up all the bricks,
Lord consecrate our kindred
Bless and make it sacred
I have seen more than I should
And I stagger to take as I could,
Am almost going blind
Please cease this ill wind
Tell them to climb the hill
And renew all their will,
So that for every cockcrow
There would be some dew
For all to stand and hearken
Not to hear and harden
It amazes me how we think
And that makes us to sink,
When we crawl and walk
We widen our mouth to talk

Nobody cares to call to order
Their intent is to cause disorder
Dear lord do not pass us by
Even if you say just good bye,
Focus and attend to my plea
Inside this overwhelming sea,
Make the devil a small toy
Let us play and have joy
Those who are born to ridicule
Never give them any bicycle
Those who cause others shame
Do not give them a name
Glad, you are not a man
Who can be regulated like a fan
Great, you see the spirit
You know the merit and demerit
Those who hate to develop
Enclose them in your envelope
For them not to be a nuisance
To your mighty substance
Shut up each and any tongue
That delights in a dirty song.

CHAPTER 45:
NEVER RELENT

Send down that your dove
Let there be a great move,
Speed up thy flight
Fly through the night,
Never stop anywhere for rest
Come and do your very best,
Lord descend for this world to unite
Give us a clean sheet to write,
If not the poor will be lost
And it will be at any cost
Very near, there is a long rope
They have produced their pope
Ready to bury anyone, righteous
You see they are too notorious,
Caring little or not about you lord
They rule this evil world,
Even when you ask us to wait
Though we are not from Kuwait
They bring up some rumour
For them to get a glamour
If you do not play a fool
They weave you like some wool
This is done in conspiracy
As they steal you like piracy,
Now I must be very plain
I had seen more than pain
So for any trouble that lingers
I must cut it off my fingers,
And those for my toes
I am removing my tight shoes
Because I see the blameless

Sleep and wake in sadness,
I repair my own tent
Yet I pay a huge rent
I wonder why I mourn
With nothing in return,
Yet none could tell
Because with them, it is well
I ask a lot of questions
But I get not even suggestions,
Life gives me headache
And it makes my heart ache
Study it and see sorrow
Whether today or tomorrow
They touch the anointed
And cut short the appointed,
Forget war and face life
Inside it, is war of strife.

CHAPTER 46:
SOW

Sow a very good crop
Even if it is a drop,
You will gather a heap
This, you must surely reap
Sometimes, you will be fought
You may even be bought
 Because money, to them is all
Whether there is a rise or fall,
The centre does not hold
When someone is not bold
So strengthen your root
Even if you are on foot,
Open your gate wide
Let it weaken the tide
I tell you, life will fade
So better now be made,
Make your own image
Mount it on the stage
So that when you are gone
It will not be undone,
If you are not a serpent
Then do not be too bent
Each time you wake up
Just fill your own cup,
Otherwise they may do it
And give you a bad bit,
Men could be mean and wicked
Their ways, very crooked
The more faithful you appear
The much evil you will bear,
Because they hate good

And eat evil like food
They hardly prefer fairness
No wonder they inflict bitterness,
Issues spring up everyday
And block some good way,
There and then we retire
Because it is not our desire
I have learnt a lot
But I have not filled my pot,
Watch those who destroy
They hardly can employ
Search for those who bind
They always lag behind,
Ask of an evil man
He is like a big ban
Never known for any feat
Instead he is just a cheat
Proof that he is fine
Then I will show his line,
He masters any trick
And uses it as a stick
Face your front and run
He has a terrible gun,
Everybody is not lovable
Because they are not approachable
Think of it when you grow
Let it give you some glow,
Life offers only just shame
Actions pour nothing but blame
Yet nothing is worthwhile
For everything is infertile,
Produce a hundred or million
You can have only a stallion
Youths leave the institution

Some do not really like it
Because they cannot benefit.

CHAPTER 47:
EXPECT SURPRISES

Hundred questions do come up
But they meet a full stop,
Then none understands the game
For all has been made lame
Tear apart your fine garment
To fast for the government
You will end up going mad
Because the rest there, are bad
Crawl far or to the middle
They will reduce you to needle,
Life is becoming a threat
The air releases much heat
Our water is no longer safe
None lives an honourable life
Stand up or sit down
Wear white or cover brown
Troubles loom here and there
Scarcity and hunger everywhere,
Watch and pray, pray and watch
Let all your dealings match
Still it has gone bad already
Just a few is willing or ready,
Teach the young where to go
They will say it is not so
Tell the old it is new
They will shout what they knew
The unborn hurries to come out

Only for him to become a tout,
See it all around the school
All is using a bad tool
They just want an ugly record
They use only a dirty word,
Because life to them is burdensome
And they want to be handsome
They drop out into the gutter
Yet wishing to have some butter,
Only a kid can think once
And never consider a rebounce
Life offers us hell and heaven
But just to whom much is given,
Sit down and write your goal
Let it never be dark like coal
Put somewhere also your will
Because you may not get your fill
Your door is open or under lock
Whatever can enter or knock,
Think and breath again
Work even if under the rain

CHAPTER 48:
BUILD

Lay a stone now or never
It may be a shelter in the river
Gold and silver which you cherish
They stay and stay and perish,
Good name lives longer than thought
Something that can never be bought
Children admire their father
 But they adore their mother,
 Nothing can stand on your path
If you want to have a bath
Bury yourself inside a grave
You can never on earth be brave,
Choose to be a commander
Not and never a pretender
I tell you again be vigilant
Also fail not to be brilliant
 It is not compulsory to eat
If it is raw or a bad meat
Another food is in the kitchen
It must not be a chicken,
Arise, O great and small
Rule, O short and tall
Tear the world very apart
Hold on to one part,
Learn and teach in it
Do not rest even one bit
Even the green bud
Will be under the mud,
If you hide it from booming
So for this keep grooming,
Because we are dashed

And all tend to be clashed.

CHAPTER 49:
IDENTITY

You must have a community
Before you can have immunity,
Even in the registry
Just like in the monastery
Sitting just on the bench
Can never teach you French,
I have observed the whether
It is heavier than the feather
Looking out from the window
Does not make one a widow,
If you can read a passage
Try and get the message
Because even another passenger
Is likely to be a messenger,
Among those in the crew
None can use a screw
This is very alarming
Even outside farming,
There is one in the missionary
He is not too ordinary
Approaching is the coronation
Everybody, prepare for the ordination,
Writing about it or felony
Tells us more of colony.

CHAPTER 50:
REALITY

I have some chocolate
It is far from surrogate
Going through spinsterhood
You learn more of sisterhood,
But any who is a bachelor
May wish to be a tailor,
Wearing a cloth like velvet
Does not make you Roosevelt,
My coach taught me a technique
I find it special and unique
Go to anywhere beyond
You cannot get the bond,
Pasting on your doorpost
'Be always on your duty post'
This is not the act of doing
Rather it is a mere saying
There is something to remember
That life did not begin in September,
The people we tend to harbour
Can add to our sweat or labour
After a severe and big threat
A lawyer cleaned off some sweat
Above the lesson, it is wonderful
That every human is fearful,
A mad man can write a note
And keep it in the remote
Those who read it can learn
Even those it does not concern,
Poverty does not bury ability
But it can affect our mentality
A wealthy man is good to go

Nothing he cannot get or do
Take always nothing but health
Everything is gone even wealth
Preferring to cook or peep
Wishing to cry or weep,
All are at some angle
Whether square or rectangle,
You can kill or catch a witch
But do not underrate a switch
The great man or centurion
Never killed even a lion,
Wonders come when we seek
They do not speak in Greek
If you set any trap
Know well your map,
Because you too can be caught
And be brought to naught

CHAPTER 51:
LOOK BEFORE YOU LEAP

Jumping off the barricade
Can land one into a brigade,
My choice is not your wish
But I have made it stylish
Let nothing be a barrier
This is a genuine carrier
After the coming age
None will live in cage,
It is either we are present
Or we are absent
Over in the height of romance
People fight for dominance
Allow the world to proceed
Someday is coming to succeed,
He is not a professor
But already a predecessor
They believe it is a wood
Therefore it can go for firewood,
My prayer is not in Latin
As I wear cotton or satin
I hope I can end the mess
That is giving a hell of stress
Nobody can go in for any
Except that one for many,
Those who eat the onion
Hardly break or quit the union
Beloved if any can get it right
He too can win all the fight
So let all of be loved
That is why I call you beloved
Yesterday I sent you on errand

I am making it a greener brand,
Trouble not any, in pain
It is enough to lose the gain
As for the food and manner
See, a different kind of banner
There is something to prevent
But not that we should invent
Below the wound is the healing
Even if it is dying or peeling
Created is man to dominate
Steady he should be to nominate
Warning has gone beyond acting
Let everybody involved be reacting,
Those who do not care
Break down like glass ware,
Men who are dedicated
Most times are delegated

CHAPTER 52:
THE PATH

If we want to be in harmony
We must not keep bad company
People who enjoy our patronage
Need not live in the parsonage
Let us rise above average
Focusing not on the vicarage
If you die for something less
You will have to remain shapeless
Allow the move you make to remain
And build your name to retain
Until we gather to discuss
We may have something to miss
Assuming we preach from a pulpit
During a meeting or summit
Listeners will never be lively
Unless the message is lovely
Whatever thing is dominant
One should see it predominant
Acting otherwise or partial
Showing anything as impartial
This gets nobody a real crown
Instead it can tear his gown
Thinking life is fake or original
Even can make one a criminal
Because emotions can rage
And look like just a mirage
This world surely must collapse
Someday when the time has, to elapse
The burden we bear are not tiny
It leaves us worn out and bony,
The lady named Mandy

Never got married to Randy
Not that they were not good
But because there were no food,
Sometimes a lot is divine
Amazingly including famine
It calls for our senses
Though we misinterpret tenses
Many do not eat snail
Yet they go to jail
Opening or uncovering a whale
May not bring up any scale,
Killing or catching a shark
Can even give you a mark
In the study of matter
Some can grow fatter
Meaning one step at a time
Also getting to the prime.

CHAPTER 53:
THE TRUTH AGAIN

Living in the municipal
Does not make one a principal
Some were there from the cradle
Yet hardly can they bridle
Select the page you will write
Make it very clean and white,
Birds live in their nest
They run from troubled breast
People have everything to forge
Forgetting someday it will purge,
Ask of the brogue kick
It differs from the goal kick,
On the topmost of the mountain
A player can fall like a captain
Walking a thousand kilometers
Covering a million centimeters
All these can cook a breakfast
And a novice will swallow it fast,
I keep warning never be in box
Otherwise you get on the crux
My thought is not on ego
Though it be like indigo,
Dreams are not improper
Even if it is a pauper
Inside a thick forest or bush
Some people still lay ambush,
Because the world has no subordinate
So they call it nothing or inordinate
There are sinners who look innocent
Some of them do bear Millicent,
Other sinners are too arrogant

And they are not ignorant
Anything that should be portrayed
Let it not at all be betrayed
For one who cannot make a reverse
Is not worthy to live in the universe,
A beautiful lady called Bridget
Hardly can make a good budget
She has twins, one is Angela
And the other is Emmanuella
She teaches them mathematics
One by one like statistics
Yet she hardly makes a difference
Because she has no confidence,
There is something extraordinary
It is nothing but the dictionary
Helping one not to oft
Making every word soft.

CHAPTER 54:
IMPERFECT

Our thoughts can err
Mostly when we interfere,
But for one to play a harp
He must be very sharp
One can make himself special
Provided his manners are crucial,
In the school of infancy
Everybody was once on tenancy
A block of flat or estate
Whoever involved paid rate,
People want to go to Pluto
As if it is a game of lido
Those who went to the mars
Still bear the witnessing scars
They are not to be prosecuted
So never have them executed,
Do not move an inch
If they want you to lynch
The likes of Thatcher
May never witness merger,
Those living in the corridor
Have nothing to hope for
You do not play hockey
With the pointer or jockey,
Every game has its rules
You can watch from any poles
It can get you excited
If it is well sited,
There are much in the village
If you have the privilege
Among the best, they breed

Is the bold and fruitful seed.
Another man called Peter
May not run a meter
His friend is always in high morale
And he keeps increasing his sale
Leave him for just one bit
He will forget about his unit
Always fighting to progress
Not thinking of the less
People learn from his character
Which he does not counter
One thing is believing in quantity
The other is going for quality,
It is not what you think
Rather what is in the link
Any person who rejects good message
Already leaves the passage.

CHAPTER 55:
FATE

The man David Livingstone
Did not build any cone
Born into this cruel earth
Yet he never cursed his birth,
You can succeed even triple
And also wear purple
But destroy not your abode
This is another success code,
Enter it and be on the move
Fly away like the dove
People will wonder and marvel
As you harden like the gravel,
Amazement would be the talk
And you will have the walk
Going away to the manicure
Returning back to the pedicure,
All these things are vanity
If we are losing our sanity,
There is a law by stipulation
However, it endures manipulation
It is a cultural heritage
Giving much more advantage
I know a handsome Polish
He is neither wise nor foolish
Whenever he is playing golf
Beside him is a golden calf
When he navigates
He also punctuates
The road he takes is amazing
Because there, animals are grazing
Anybody who is very efficient

Engaging him may be sufficient,
Look not down on your employer
Else he becomes a player
Look out for best employee
Though he be an amputee,
Make it yourself a soap jelly
It gives you no pot belly
Unless you have a tally
You may lose the rally,
After learning how to do good
Then make it your everyday food
A day without a righteous act
Can make you lose a rare contract,
Tell him that we are in winter
Let all rest including the hunter
Carrying a gun like double barrel
Is not a guarantee to kill a squirrel
It can be used on a rodent
If one is not that prudent
On it was pasted a logo
But it was carrying a cargo
He is a big time fraudster
That is why he is a monster,
It may be forbidden to eat Melon
When we planted only watermelon,
I doubt if he takes vegetable
Because to him, it is not palatable.
My dog is named Imbecile
This makes him look fragile,
To overuse the cane
Makes one inhumane
It can keep one in bondage
And make him use bandage
To one who is an agriculturist

He can too be a horticulturist
Provided he is not a quark
Who causes harm like shark,
An archbishop who cannot convince
Should not Mann the province
For he will ruin the cathedral
Trying to start his remedial.

CHAPTER 56:
TAKE HEED

Men should run away from liquor
So that they do not get to stupor
This can never be of Michael
Neither will it be about Ezekiel
These men were very noble
And it made them bubble
Try working with a robot
The work will be very hot,
It does not mean you will slack
Because you are the one at the back,
To Mann any kind of machine
You must learn how to shine
For life does not blow
When you refuse to flow,
Talk of what we learnt of recent
Stop dreaming of Millicent
Things we see come and fade
Never do they remain on parade,
Such is life and what it has
It diffuses and evaporates like gas,
At the prime age of thirty
One should be preparing for forty
Otherwise it will hit like a wave
And nothing would one seem to have
Write a song in the morning
Learn it well before evening,
Never go to bed empty handed
Else you will wake up stranded,
The food we eat is not all
So wake up to the clarion call
The dress we put on is not us

Rather talks of our our focus
Let what we do be our passion
If we must retain our portion,
Fighting to be loved is fake
It means you have no stake
Love comes from the bone
Piercing through every stone,
Paying to win is very rude
It tells you can go too nude
Winning, that is by merit
Can hardly go into debit,
So let us all be careful
Let our world too be peaceful
Revenge is not important
Sure, it will never be reluctant
For nature does carter for all
Even those who were made to fall.

CHAPTER 57:
FAKERY

The love we preach is ill
It does not come at will
Rather we force it to lust
And cook it when not we must,
We cheat ourselves happily
Dressing our wounds shabbily
It is written on our fore
Following us from shore to shore
Pretence can never heal any
But it can expose too many
Besides there is a big hurt
Finding it difficult to cut short,
As we try to run or escape
The more we take the sour grape
Any who can successful return
Will be saved from the burn
Listen, a giant is not god
He too can be beaten with the rod
A teacher is not a spirit
He can also fail the sit.
Those we look up to can disappear
They too can be made to reappear
But men are quick and judgmental
Even when they all are going mental
Some who want to retire
Tie themselves with a wire
They even jump from the roof
Only trying to show a proof
That they are no longer interested
So they crave to be rested,
Picking under the table some crumb

Does not give you power to go dumb,
Let it be known to each student
That it pays to be prudent
Parents will not die for their children
Be they the Sanhedrin,
The world, we are yet to describe
Because in it also is the scribe
Only God knows what it is
For it is His alone and only His,
Stop the brag, son of mortal
You who are wickedly brutal
Put on your garment of wickedness
And live on it, abject bitterness
Until your saviour gives you freedom
You remain in dark kingdom,
Pray that He comes very quick
I see you go down sick.

CHAPTER 58:
COMPARE

For men who are hard to satisfy
Check them they easily crucify
They can always import
But never will export,
Try the easy going man
He rotates just like the fan
Not too hard to regulate
Admiring all to congratulate
Anywhere he breaks down
He releases his crown
Unlike the other who possesses
Not giving room for new dresses,
Jump to hell, it is your job
You will be beaten by a mob
He can die for his business
Even in his big laziness,
Go along with a superior
He will not make you inferior
But if you meet a lord
Be ready to lose your chord,
When they lose your hand
They realize how small their band
Then they know the things taken for granted
Indeed are not and never will be granted
There is something about the moisture
Sometimes, it retains the texture
That is if given the chance
And allowed a time to enhance,
A people yet unborn do not die
But we and they can have a tie
It is not bad to do a joke

Believing it will not be a stroke
On the hand it is barbaric
If it has to be very satanic,
Left alone nobody can be
Even the small busy bee
At the verge of being nice
Anybody can be a prince,
Provided you are at the top gear
With less or nothing to bear
Hit the hammer on the engine
It is a part of the marine,
Mind you, always be gallant
And be ready as well as combatant
A fighter who fears his opponent
Would be captured like a rodent,
In the land of the trainers
All are great and gainers
If you fail the government
You will not be given assignment,
Understandable and simple
It can be used as an example
When we fail to obey instruction
We may head for destruction,
Let us encourage each other
For our strength lies in one another
There will be a new dawn someday
And we will forget the tragic yesterday,
It will be a new life of plenty
Nobody will be empty
No more shall we run from the caterpillar
Because firmly ours shall be the pillar,
Going for a great battle
Never requires any wattle
For it is only the stamp

Which will not cramp,
If the world has made you a keeper
Please do not go for the cheaper
Especially when it gives you a chair
Make sure it is free and fair
Everybody cannot understand a notice
Mostly one who is poor or a novice.

CHAPTER 59:
MAKE A MOVE

Lying down on the tile
Makes none agile
Standing tall on the marble
Makes nobody become humble
Crawling on the bare floor
Does not open the door,
Kneeling daily on the altar
In repentance, makes things alter
But all these will be done away
When the Holy Ghost leads the way.
A bird knows her nest
So should man know his chest
A king rules his kingdom
So shall a star man his stardom
Up there are heroes past
Down here are captains last,
None chooses his glory or crown
Whether green, blue or brown
For awhile, troubles will cease
And love for peace will increase
Dwelling in great darkness
Sleeping in deep sadness
Waking in big toil and task
Will be what nobody will ask,
On the front pages of newspaper
Are the pictures of a skyscraper
It is just there for fancy
Maybe to call for some fantasy
It will be a little for an introvert
If you finally make him a convert
These people are not in the mood

So they can easily be misunderstood
What they have is strange
But it can bring much change
Never undermine them for anything
For it can make you lose something
When they are hard to harness
Put them on little recess
Here, you can put them up
And have them fill the cup
Only a little and they are caught
They can take away the draught,
Never take it for pride
As it can roll on the tide,
Push more and open the gate
You and they are on date
 Before awhile, it is begun
They will help set the sun.

CHAPTER 60:
THE FACT

By the left is an ankle
By the right is an uncle
It is walking in the front
Moving closer to a fount,
So he then is lifted
Because he is gifted
In the house of a polygamist
Is a well known journalist,
His flare is in criminology
Being helped by psychology
It is good to be a go getter
Even under a patched shelter
Make use of your accelerator
Do not destroy your calibrator,
Life is a make and break
Once awhile it applies brake,
Always listen to your tutor
He is also your own mentor
Firing when you should quit
Has already made you unfit,
A good work on the ledger
Must tell about a merger,
Otherwise something is missing
Which would keep you hissing,
My point is not neutral
For it is not also periodical
An old and ancient train
Still has its coach and chain
It will always run on the rail
Just as the ship would sail,
In the world of harsh survival

We face secret or open rival
Where no one can really be in harmony
Even in the so called matrimony
You can be a good musician
And also a wonderful politician
All these do not give rest
Rather you become a guest
Under the pillow of a pastor
Are sounds of the traitor
His lips are as green as pasture
But unconcerned about rapture
In the hit of a low star
It moves like a speeding car
If you do not hold your clutch
You will give someone a punch,
This may land you in jail
If you are not granted bail

CHAPTER 61:
CAUTION

Looking before you leap
 It is not costly but cheap
For one is like the sunlight
And the other like the moonlight,
A home of foolish occupants
Is a house for infants
Paying to steal the ballot
Keeps one to suffer a lot
Though they are signing autograph
And be plotting high towering graph,
The issue is not the longitude
But the chances of ending, rude
Oppose the ugly motion
They rob you like lotion
It does not pay to be ugly
Instead to stay all godly
In the land of Ethiopia
They also know onomatopoeia
What happens in Uganda
Does not stop in Rwanda,
The people of Columbia
Also travel to Namibia
In the ancient city of Benin
Anybody can start or begin,
Whether it is called a cankerworm
Or baptized an earthworm
It can surge and destroy
Reducing a man to a boy,
If you allow a discovery
You will enjoy some recovery,
Inside the human skull is brain

It holds the body like a chain,
Some people do not eat yam
But they eat much of ram,
Following them is not a crime
Even if you do not take lime
On the contrary, is a class
That eats anything in mass
Study them, they are normal
Authentic, real and original,
Gather the yoke of a goat
Bear it and stay afloat
You may not reach your destination
No matter your angle of inclination,
A teacher who joins a cult
Knows not much of the result,
There is more to life than we know
Unfortunately we allow it freeze like snow.

CHAPTER 62:
REMEMBER

The world is a global village
Making a big and soft tillage,
Understanding this will help men
For them not to die like hen,
A few has good understanding
Many cannot endure standing
Any man without opposition
Is not useful like preposition,
Count your success and failure
At least one can keep you secure
You can get to Mount Everest
It does not make you the richest
Unless you have tasted poverty
You can believe it is a fraternity,
On the air hover many chances
Filled with contaminated substances
Indeed it is very tremendous
But many make it callous
Never think it must be annual
For things can make it continual,
One was born on eighteenth May
He has all it takes to play
Needing not to form a fist
With a clean list,
The other was born in April
With the ability to drill
Another was born in January
Doing so well in binary
Many people who came last
Mostly do not end in a blast
As you can control a furnace

So they can clean the surface,
A miner must not be rich
But he can suffer a big stitch
In the early hours of creation
There was a great real protection
As unfortunate as a betrayal
As hopeful as a renewal,
On the wake of slave trade
Some homes were also made
Bitterly to some they were severed
And sadly a lot was hindered
All these make us uncomfortable
Especially now the world is unstable,
Like life elsewhere it was stupid
Because the terrors were solid,
For any who survived that ache
It was a continuous headache.

CHAPTER 63:
CHANGE IS INEVITABLE

They said in that era
There was no camera
From what we see today
We could imagine yesterday,
To lord yourself over others
Does not tell of mothers
Because they are soft and tender
Having the powers of a mender,
The story is just wickedness
As some live in bitterness
Nobody can survive alone
No matter how golden his throne,
We have failed to note this
Thinking we can retire in bliss
Some friends who drink rum
Have their souls to gum,
Stepping down to the gallows
Knowing not what he swallows,
One of them is called Dennis
He likes to play tennis
Going instead for a field event
With prayers that are fervent
One, would not pass
That whose heart is made of brass.
Living in a well known slum
Never can grant anyone asylum
Even a dirty and devilish fortress
Will not and cannot undo the stress,
They can succeed with their blindfold
But someday everything will unfold,
Professing to be a Christian

Should not make one a barbarian
Others know well their religion
But they abhor and mess the tradition,
A world of roses equally fade
Even to the poorest grade
Anyone who does not use a protractor
Is not qualified to be a contractor,
For he cannot know hereabout
After being cautioned or given a shout.
Teach him about a compass
Also help him get a good pass
You just gave him a digger
Making things for him bigger,
Fill his bag with money
He will leak you like honey
Help to safeguard his purse
He cannot work as a nurse,
If you are wearing your boot
You may wish to go on foot
This may not be the only way
But because you want to make hay,
Everybody is an indigene
As normal as an aborigine,
A landlord on the coast
May be a tenant at the toast
You can play in the mud
But never with the bud
For we look up for a vegetation
At least for the next generation,
If one could rule over the peer
He will have himself to cheer
Because life is dependent on mistakes
Assuming one wasted all his cakes,
A little while it will be quick

Even unto a growing chick
Anything that is maternal
Does not avoid the paternal,
Things we love may be danger
Calling deeply for an avenger
But how do we know the wrath
When we cannot estimate the worth.

CHAPTER 64:
IT COULD BE YOU

Like other men he was born
But with a different horn
His heart is very poor
Yet unlocking every door,
He is not in government
Instead on a big assignment
He did not attend college
But full of knowledge
He defends no university
Rather he masters adversity,
He eats with no silver spoon
But lights the earth like moon
He has written a page
That can never be in cage
A good friend to the needy
Sharing whatever he has
Diffusing far, near like gas
A word from him is better
It can never become bitter,
Planting everywhere with change
Making the world look strange.
Jesus taught us the same
But we play just game
Societal men come to drink
They join, forming a link
Sending therefore a message
That opens a fresh passage
He is moving in a boat
Keeping everyone afloat
Questions get answered
Fears also get conquered

Our walk is not carnal
But we chase it from canal
He understands the law
So he follows it raw
Working in the lord's vine
Because he is very divine,
Life has its principle
It does not taste like apple
He knows when to quit
And also when to knit
Having in mind a goal
Instead of mining coal.

CHPTER 65:
FOOD FOR THOUGHT
(A)
Tsunami can sink Miami
Pope can be caught by the rope
Supermodel may not be a role model
Resistance equals not the distance
Bed can be red,
Manners are banners
Carriers can be barriers
Strangers can be messengers
Crooks can write books
Sound makes you found,
Saint can also faint
Guilt can never sustain the built
Lone soul equals dry bone,
Thunder puts all asunder
Smoke causes choke
Turn right to return.
Task the mask
Trouble can come double
Angels may live parallel,
Boom may need extra room
Mental awareness should be instrumental
Liver can be lost in the river
Sanity outlives insanity
Coach must not be a cockroach
Age never hides in the cage
Sweetness comes with bitterness
Misuse is abuse
Learning goes with discerning
Nebraska differs from Alaska
Curse affects the purse
Commit to submit

Brands manifest on lands
Invest no matter the harvest,
Opinions are companions
Rest comes after test
Subject is never perfect.
Alas, use well the atlas
Groundnut can be used as kola nut
Blame is nobody's name
Designation can bring resignation

(B)
Agony can make life an irony
Harmony brings testimony
Trowel can travel
Flair should fly in the air
Clash can come from being harsh
Brush cannot clean the bush
Toast can build the coast,
Favour attracts flavour
Distraction can bring destruction
Suggestion needs digestion
Optimism wards off pessimism
Magnet ceases signet
Maturity goes along with purity
Unusual to remain casual
Scandals should not be worn as sandals
Sheet can contain a fleet
Tissue can become an issue
Peg should not be on the leg,
Sick man can design a wick
Maggot fears no pot
Utensil can be drawn with pencil
Clementina is a sister to Augustina
Virginia can live in Georgina

Fustina lives with Justina
Rosemary may not know Mary
Surprise serves also as an advice
Notice is good for a novice.
Popularity is not charity
Feather gets wet by wheather
Tin can come from within
Insurance is not total assurance
Mayor is not guaranteed a major
Donor may not be minor
Senior was once a junior
Orange is not strange.
Oval is not naval
Tape may never get the shape
Pianist could be rapist
General can be suicidal
Seat can be a feat.
Defeat can come from a cheat
Power comes from the tower
Flowers can gives showers

(C)
Arthur may never concur
Laziness can bring messiness
Stupidity also extends to nudity
Senses also give wrong sentences
Personalities make no abilities
Sources decide resources
Summon can be common
Game is never the same
Chalk can do a walk
Puberty is not liberty
God can break any rod.
Adder can climb the ladder

151

Scoundrel can die like squirrel
Thorn can be on the horn
Elephant can keep a covenant,
Rejoice to hear your voice
Boot can spoil a root
Diversity is not an adversity
Shell may not allow your bell
Alarm can do some harm
Charm cannot sustain a farm,
Inside is what we can offer outside
Reasons fail in some seasons
Flags can become rags
Coat fits no goat
Boat must be afloat
Rains come with gains
Care must be made flare
Broom sweeps away doom
Dove is always on the move
Staggering can be shattering
Cuddle the hurdle
Oracles dismantle obstacles
Miracle is at the pinnacle
Arise and be wise
Lift up your gift
Shift and make your legs swift,
Consecrate yourself, be not late
Wills climb hills
Serene can be the scene,
Agent can be an pungent
Identification is personification

   (D)
Milk is not silk

Weak, you can lose the peak
Tomorrow can bring sorrow
Parent needs to be transparent
Richards mean no orchards
Bastards can play good cards
Water is a wonderful matter
Saving is waving
Ahead, if you want to be the head
Unlock the stock
Gold is always bold
Susanna loves banana
Vegetable is perishable
Dynasty must not be nasty,
Apple is not nipple
Some are not handsome
Stardom follows kingdom
Wisdom handles boredom
Secret does not remain concrete
Liquid can go solid
Rude is crude
Flute can never remain mute
Keeping calm may cause weeping
Solace may not be in palace
Minder can be a reminder,
Contact may not be in contract
Sunset can be caused by mindset,
Dreams do not flow like streams
Beams can be raised by teams
Deacon should be a beacon
Cracks can still be tracks
Back your sack
Incentive can also make one insensitive
Lake can bring some shake
Fake never equals good make,

Deal carries seal
Meal may not heal
Congregation should know no segregation
Bondage does terrible damage,
Sabotage is a hostage
Subterfuge is not a refuge
Arrogance is no assistance,
Patience lives in the conscience.

(E)
Talent should not be hidden
Religion is a scorpion
Region is full of legion
Professionalism is devoid of egotism,
Technique should be unique
Thunder puts things asunder
Balm can bring calm
Joke can poke
Coldness buries boldness
Link can be pink
Sensitivity can avert calamity,
Pierce can be fierce
Wink can sink
Tamed, you can be named
Vigilant can make one combatant
Brave, you can save
Calculative, you become more creative
Articulated, you become more coordinated
Right, you can carry on in light
Bright, you Mann your flight.
Sweat and climb great
Composed, you must be opposed
Unborn cannot be stubborn

Peer can turn a deer
Cheer, if you are a volunteer
Crime is against time
Lover should not be undercover.
Anchor should not be in rancour
Recession can bring dispossession
Mildness goes with childishness.

Publisher's list

If you have enjoyed The *Rhythm of Life* consider these other fine books from Mwanaka Media and Publishing:

Cultural Hybridity and Fixity by Andrew Nyongesa
The Water Cycle by Andrew Nyongesa
Tintinnabulation of Literary Theory by Andrew Nyongesa
I Threw a Star in a Wine Glass by Fethi Sassi
South Africa and United Nations Peacekeeping Offensive Operations by Antonio Garcia
Africanization and Americanization Anthology Volume 1, Searching for Interracial, Interstitial, Intersectional and Interstates Meeting Spaces, Africa Vs North America by Tendai R Mwanaka
A Conversation..., A Contact by Tendai Rinos Mwanaka
A Dark Energy by Tendai Rinos Mwanaka
Africa, UK and Ireland: Writing Politics and Knowledge Production Vol 1 by Tendai R Mwanaka
Best New African Poets 2017 Anthology by Tendai R Mwanaka and Daniel Da Purificacao
Keys in the River: New and Collected Stories by Tendai Rinos Mwanaka
Logbook Written by a Drifter by Tendai Rinos Mwanaka
Mad Bob Republic: Bloodlines, Bile and a Crying Child by Tendai Rinos Mwanaka
How The Twins Grew Up/Makurire Akaita Mapatya by Milutin Djurickovic and Tendai Rinos Mwanaka
Writing Language, Culture and Development, Africa Vs Asia Vol 1 by Tendai R Mwanaka, Wanjohi wa Makokha and Upal Deb
Zimbolicious Poetry Vol 1 by Tendai R Mwanaka and Edward Dzonze

Ashes by Ken Weene and Omar O Abdul

Ouafa and Thawra: About a Lover From Tunisia by Arturo Desimone

Thoughts Hunt The Loves/Pfungwa Dzinovhima Vadiwa by Jeton Kelmendi

وَالغَمَام...ويَسهَرُ اللَّيْلُعَلَىشَفَتِي by Fethi Sassi

A Letter to the President by Mbizo Chirasha

Righteous Indignation by Jabulani Mzinyathi:

This is Not a Poem by Richard Inya

Soon to be released

Notes From a Modern Chimurenga: Collected Stories by Tendai Rinos Mwanaka

Tom Boy by Megan Landman

My Spiritual Journey: A Study of the Emerald Tablets by Jonathan Thompson

Blooming Cactus by Mikateko Mbambo

School of Love and Other Stories by Ricardo Felix Rodriguez

Cycle of Life by Ikegwu Michael Chukwudi

Denga reshiri yokunze kwenyika by Fethi Sassi

Because Sadness is Beautiful by Tanaka Chidora

PHENOMENOLOGY OF DECOLONIZING THE UNIVERSITY: Essays in the Contemporary Thoughts of Afrikology by Zvikomborero Kapuya

INFLUENCE OF CLIMATE VARIABILITY ON THE PREVALENCE OF DENGUE FEVER IN MANDERA COUNTY, KENYA by NDIWA JOSEPH KIMTAI

https://facebook.com/MwanakaMediaAndPublishing/

Printed in the United States
By Bookmasters